Series / Number 07-042

MW00764477

USING PUBLISHED DATA

Errors and Remedies

HERBERT JACOB
University of Wisconsin, Madison

SAGE PUBLICATIONS
The International Professional Publishers
Newbury Park   London   New Delhi

The author gratefully acknowledges permission granted by the following to quote from their works. For the quotation from Gordon, page 25: Reprinted with permission of the author from THE PUBLIC INTEREST, No. 63 (Spring 1981), p. 128. © 1981 by National Affairs, Inc. For the quotation from Morgenstern, page 27: From Oskar Morgenstern, *On the Accuracy of Economic Observations,* 2nd edn, completely revised. Copyright 1950, © 1963 by Princeton University Press. Excerpt. For the quotation from Simon, page 49: From Julian L. Simon, *Basic Research Methods in Social Science,* Second Edition. Copyright by Random House, Inc.

For information address:

SAGE Publications, Inc.
2455 Teller Road
Newbury Park, California 91320
E-mail: order@sagepub.com

SAGE Publications Ltd.
6 Bonhill Street
London EC2A 4PU
United Kingdom

SAGE Publications India Pvt. Ltd.
M-32 Market
Greater Kailash I
New Delhi 110 048 India

Printed in the United States of America

International Standard Book Number 0-8039-2299-X

Library of Congress Catalog Card No. L.C. 84-050250

99   00   01   15   14   13   12   11   10

When citing a university paper, please use the proper form. Remember to cite the Sage University Paper series title and include the paper number. One of the following formats can be adapted (depending on the style manual used):

(1) JACOB, HERBERT. (1984) Using published data: Errors and remedies. Sage University Paper Series on Quantitative Applications in the Social Sciences, 07-042. Newbury Park, CA: Sage.

OR

(2) Jacob, H. (1984). *Using published data: Errors and remedies* (Sage University Paper Series on Quantitative Applications in the Social Sciences, series no. 07-042). Newbury Park, CA: Sage.

CONTENTS

Series Editor's Introduction

Professor Jacob's manuscript is a clearly stated and interesting guide to the uses and abuses of published data. As the number of publicly available social science data sets grows substantially, scholars are increasingly prone to use data sets to analyze research questions that did not occur to those who actually collected the data in the first place. Certainly, for advanced undergraduate and graduate students forced to produce a research paper or thesis under severe constraints of time and available resources, the analysis of data from the public domain is a virtual necessity.

Very often—perhaps most often—scholars who analyze published data are prone to ignore the kinds of problems discussed by Professor Jacob. By publishing this guide, it is the hope of the editors and publishers of this series to alert budding scholars to the rather serious problems of sampling, of reliability, and of validity that can plague even the best available data sets. More than simple awareness, however, Professor Jacob suggests possible solutions to the problems engendered by this type of analysis, and where solutions are not easily available, he suggests the appropriate cautions that authors must publicly state. His advice is also, occasionally, that the scholar abandon the project rather than publish potentially misleading results.

I am particularly pleased to add this manuscript to our list of publications because more than anything else it forces the now proud and occasionally arrogant quantitative social scientist to re-learn just a tad of humility. We have increasingly come to view measurement errors and related problems within the framework of sophisticated quantitative statistical techniques. Distinctions among design, measurement, and analysis have recently been blurred in the social sciences, and I for one have tended to view this as a healthy development. The research process is indeed a single, holistic enterprise, and a weak link at any point along

5

the entire way can very easily invalidate our substantive conclusions. Recent developments in social science methodology have tended to emphasize this fundamental truth.

But I think that, as is inevitably true, every advance has its related costs. My own view is that the costs of recent developments in the analysis of measurement errors are at least twofold. First, problems of measurement are now often viewed as merely technical, to be solved largely by the application of powerful statistical techniques. This has, I think, caused many social scientists to relax their standards for data collection and for the use of published sources of data. If data are plagued by some sort of measurement error, random or nonrandom, we merely incorporate that into our measurement models and feel just a bit smug that now "that is taken care of." Professor Jacob reminds us that unless we are intimately familiar with the substantive nature of the problem we wish to analyze, we are unlikely to understand the nature of the errors incorporated in our data and most certainly cannot "correct for" these errors. Additionally, we must have a great deal of familiarity not only with the substance of the problem, but with the details of data collection procedures used by all sources of published data.

A related cost of recent advances in the analysis of measurement errors flows from the increasing popularity of the view that measurement can be handled largely as a problem of analysis rather than of conceptualization or substance. This has led many researchers to believe that once they have mastered the technical details of measurement and of the general linear model, they are prepared to deal effectively with almost any social science subject matter. "Have gun, will travel" may not be far from the mark in characterizing—or perhaps caricaturing—the most enthusiastic among us. We can travel at will from subject matter to subject matter, confident that our contribution will be lasting because we will not make egregious mistakes of data analysis or of measurement. Absent detailed knowledge of substance and of data collection, this confidence is unwarranted. Professor Jacob's work should do much to shake that confidence.

Although the above view may be overstated, Professor Jacob clearly demonstrates through ample use of examples that social scientists who analyze published data without a great deal of detailed knowledge do so not only at great risk to themselves, but also to their colleagues who will take their substantive conclusions very seriously. This is particularly true of scholars whose statistical analysis is sophisticated and flawless, thus enhancing the credibility of their conclusions. Yet, if insufficient attention is paid to the concerns expressed by Professor Jacob, erroneous conclusions will result in spite of our best efforts.

Exhortation aside, this monograph is meant to serve as a guide for advanced undergraduates and for beginning graduate students who face the use of secondary data without any notion of the potential pitfalls that await them. It is not a checklist for them, which if followed will ensure that they avoid the problems enumerated herein. Such a list is misleading, if not impossible to construct. Rather, this monograph is meant to illustrate the sorts of potential glitches the scholar ought to expect in the analysis of published data, and the general strategies that ought to be employed in detecting and adjusting one's analysis for these glitches. I also urge my colleagues to consider seriously the issues raised here, because they tend to be the sorts of problems we note in the work of others but tend to ignore, at least publicly, in our own efforts.

–John L. Sullivan
Series Co-Editor

USING PUBLISHED DATA
Errors and Remedies

HERBERT JACOB
University of Wisconsin, Madison

INTRODUCTION

Libraries and computerized data archives are bursting with data ready to be analyzed. They hold thousands of statistical reports published by U.S. government agencies in addition to the reports from United Nations agencies and foreign governments. Moreover, private data collections are often readily available either in published form or by connecting to a computerized data bank.

These data are like the apple in the Garden of Eden: tempting but full of danger. Although the data are often published in formats that suggest that they are authoritative and trustworthy, they are almost always riddled with errors of one sort or another. This essay seeks to alert the unwary researcher of some of the pitfalls in using them. I shall set out both the problems and some remedies. Readers should not be discouraged. For almost every problem there is a solution or at worst an acceptable compromise. It will sometimes seem that the dangers outrun the remedies; that should give us pause as we undertake research based on these data or rely on analyses that use such sources. But it need not paralyze our research.

1. SAMPLES, CENSUSES, AND SAMPLING ERROR

The data one finds in publications are counts of one sort or another, which for many reasons may be incorrect. They may come from com-

AUTHOR'S NOTE: *This paper is the outgrowth of many discussions with Robert L. Lineberry and the substantial assistance of Michael J. Rich. I also benefited greatly from suggestions on an earlier draft by several anonymous referees; by John Sullivan; and by my colleagues, Tom Cook, Andrew Gordon, Alex Hicks, Kenneth Janda, and Wesley Skogan. None of them, however, bears any responsibility for its contents.*

plete counts or from partial counts. The U.S. Decennial Census is the best example of a data source that claims to be a complete count. It purports to be a total count of all persons living in the United States at a particular time. Vote counts are another example; they purport to be a count of all ballots in an election. Partial counts claim to represent a larger population or universe. The best such partial count is a random, probability sample. A simple random sample is a partial count in which each element of the whole population has an equal chance of being included and every combination of elements in the population has an equal chance. Those elements chosen are selected randomly (Kish, 1965; Warwick and Lininger, 1975; Selltiz et al., 1976: 522). Many variations of the random, probability sample exist. Some seek to stratify the sample according to known characteristics of the population; others seek to cluster the points from which the data will be collected. Many samples, however, are not based on the principles of random selection. Quota samples, for instance, choose data to fill a quota that reflects known traits of the population. Other collections are simply based on convenience. Observations are included because they happened to be available when the researchers went looking for their data.

The distinction between random samples and other collections of data is crucial because of the errors that all data collections contain. Sometimes these errors flow from the ways in which samples are selected; we call that sampling error. In other cases, the errors result from inadequacies in the measurement process; we call those measurement errors. Most of this essay deals with various kinds of measurement errors. However, we should first confront the possibility of sampling error and the steps we may take to overcome it.

Sampling error can be easily estimated *only* when one is working with data collected through a random sample. Two statistical theorems provide us with the tools for such an estimate. The *law of large numbers* states that with a large number of samples, the mean of the sample means will equal the mean of the population. The *central limit theorem* states that if we draw numerous large samples, the means of those samples will approximate the bell-shaped curve of the normal distribution (Palumbo, 1977: 276). These two theorems permit us to estimate both the mean and a point of a distribution with the formula:

$$u = \bar{X} + Z \ \frac{s}{\sqrt{\ }}$$

where

- Z is the point under the normal curve of a standardized distribution corresponding to a selected confidence interval. It takes on the values of + or – 1.96 for a 95% confidence interval and a value of + or – 2.58 for a 99% confidence interval;
- s is the sample variance;
- n is the number of cases in the sample.

Let us suppose that we wish to estimate the mean age of unemployed persons in some city for a given year. If we obtain the information from a random sample of 500 persons and find from it that the sample mean is 35 and the sample variance is 2.5, our estimate of the reliability of the mean age of 35 with a 95% confidence is

$$35 + \text{or} - 1.96(2.5/\text{sqrt}500) \text{ or}$$

$$35 + \text{or} - 1.96(2.5/22.4) \text{ or}$$

$$35 + \text{or} - .22$$

A 99% confidence interval in this instance would be

$$35 + \text{or} - .29$$

Note that these estimates provide a margin of error. The more certain we wish to be of our estimate, the larger the confidence interval will be. For example, were we to estimate the number of smokers in a population from a random sample with a confidence of being correct 99% of the time, we would have a larger error range than if we were satisfied with a 95% chance of being correct. In some instances, the confidence interval allows us to conclude that the estimate we have obtained is insignificant because the estimated error is much larger than the estimate itself. In other cases, the confidence interval is so large that the estimate is useless. For instance, in the 1983 Chicago mayoral campaign, a last minute public opinion poll showed one candidate leading by 52% of the vote against his opponent's 48%, but the margin of error was estimated as + or – 6 percent. Such an inexact estimate is of little help in predicting the outcome (WMFT, April 11, 1983 newscast; same poll reported without error estimate in Chicago Tribune [1983]).

The ability to estimate error is a very important characteristic of random samples. One never knows whether or not a particular estimate is correct, but using a random sample allows one to estimate the probability that the estimate is wrong. Confidence in sample data is, therefore, always modified by a concrete estimate of the chance that the data are incorrect. Consequently, almost every publication of data based on samples should carry with it a discussion of the error estimate. Many reports based on samples now do so.

By contrast, when data are collected by some nonrandom procedure, no such statistical estimates of sampling error are possible. One can be certain that errors exist, but one does not know how large they might be or what the probability is for a given error range. In addition, because the data collection did not use random selection procedures, the errors may not be symmetrically arranged around the mean. They may all be clustered at one end of the distribution or another, and one can never know what direction the errors will take. For instance, the error may be larger in rural than urban areas or the reverse may be true; minorities may be overcounted or undercounted; too many or too few voters may appear in the data base. There is no way of accurately estimating such biases in nonrandom samples.

Our inability to specify sampling error occurs with both nonrandom samples like a television call-in poll and full counts like the census. They are full of selection errors, the extent of which we cannot estimate with any statistical reliability. Only when one is counting a very small group that is directly under close observation, can one have confidence in the results. For instance, I can know with considerable confidence how many students are enrolled in a small seminar. Those not present on any given day can be easily traced; I am made aware of those who drop. That is not true for my large lecture classes. When I teach more than 200 students, I never know how many are actually enrolled in the course. Some are absent every day because of illness; some miss tests. Some will drop without telling me, and others will enter the course. Even the listing that the registrar provides will often be inaccurate. At the very end of the semester, I can report the number of students for whom I have complete grades, but often one or two students will announce themselves as having been present for part of the course and eligible for a final grade.

Such difficulties are multiplied a thousandfold for a national census. It is well known that many persons are missed by such a census—

because they failed to fill out a form, were never contacted by a census worker, lived in an area considered too dangerous for census workers to go to, or were in transit. Middle-class white Americans who live stable lives are most easily counted by the census. They can be reached at a known address, are able to read the census form, and feel an obligation to return it. That is not equally true for members of many minority groups. Blacks have been consistently undercounted both because many are more suspicious of government agents and because they are more difficult to reach than white middle-class Americans. Hispanics present a still different problem because some of them are illegal aliens who fear that being counted by the census might endanger their continued residence in the United States (even though census records are not available to immigration or other law enforcement agencies). Still other persons are confused by census questions about their ethnicity. In states where few Hispanics are reported to live, sizable numbers of people misidentified themselves as Hispanic in the 1980 census. In the words of a census official, "Apparently many people did not know what a Mexican-American was, spotted the 'Amer.' on the form and marked it, even though we had American abbreviated and squeezed in between Mexican and Chicano" (New York Times, 1983).

Because of such problems, population counts are always somewhat incorrect. They contain greater errors for some groups (e.g., blacks and Hispanics) than for others (U.S. Congress, Subcommittee on Census, 1977, 1980a). Custom and legal precedent lead government publications to display figures down to the last whole number. In fact, the numbers have a margin of error that may be as high as 5 percent. The result is that "complete" counts may be less reliable than random samples! Both are certain to have errors, but the sampling error in random samples can be estimated with a high degree of accuracy, whereas the selection error in full counts can only be guessed at.

These problems, however, do not present insuperable barriers to the productive use of published statistics, even when we are not told the margin of error or when the data are supposed to be complete counts. Where the data come from random samples, one must often search further for information about sampling error. The data one finds in published sources such as the *Statistical Abstract of the United States* (U.S. Bureau of the Census, 1981, 1982-83) are often extracted from exhaustive studies that include much information about sampling error.

Consequently, one needs to go to the original source that is cited in the *Statistical Abstract*; sometimes that source will send the reader to other technical publications that provide estimates of sampling error. It is a trip worth taking.

Data that are not collected by a random probability sample cannot be evaluated in the same way. In the case of the U.S. Census, detailed technical studies exist that examine undercounts and overcounts; these are based on an analysis of the internal consistency of responses to census questions, on comparisons with recounts, and on comparisons with random sample data for the same populations. Such studies provide careful researchers with considerable information about the likely scope of counting error. For most other counts, however, no such studies exist. Nevertheless, there is another remedy. Many data based on a full count are reported down to the last digit. For instance, the 1970 population of Sacramento, California is reported to have been 257,105 (U.S. Bureau of the Census, 1977: 624). We can be reasonably certain that the population in fact was around 250,000, but we have no idea whether it was 259,872 or 252,307. For most uses, it makes little difference, although if Sacramento qualified as a first-class city under state law when it surpassed a quarter-million population, the addition or subtraction of a few inhabitants could have serious consequences.

The problem is more complicated when one uses population counts in cross-national analyses. Some nations schedule census counts as regularly as the United States and have counting procedures that are as good as or better than those in the United States. In many nations, however, census counts are occasional events; such countries lack the bureaucratic machinery to organize accurate counts. In more than a few instances, population statistics are politically sensitive, and regimes have a stake in overestimating or underestimating particular ethnic groups or other components of the population. Population counts and estimates may be found in the official publications of individual nations, in UNESCO reports, and in the *World Handbook of Political and Social Indicators* (Russet et al., 1964; Taylor and Hudson, 1972). The World Handbook provides some information about potential sources of error. Moreover, it estimates the size of the error margin for each country. For instance, for the United States, it reports an error margin for the 1965 population estimate of 2%; by contrast, the error margin for

Saudi Arabia is 30.8% (Taylor and Hudson, 1972: 295, 296). Understanding the significance of these numbers, however, requires careful reading of the text and the notes that accompany the table; indeed, the table itself does not even indicate the year for which the population is given. Careful reading is always a prerequisite for use of published statistics.

The error estimates provided by the *World Handbook* are an example of a rule of thumb that may be used to mitigate excessive specificity in full counts. Where specific error estimates do not exist, we must turn to other stopgap measures. One such expedient is to take advantage of the fact that many government publications round population counts to the nearest 1000. That does not merely save space on the printed page but also reflects skepticism about the last digit accuracy of the numbers. It calls the reader's attention to the likelihood that the numbers are not fully accurate. The consequence of such a precaution is to minimize small differences that may well be the result of error rather than reflecting a difference in the true occurrence of whatever it is we are studying. The precise degree of rounding will depend on the character of the data. With very large numbers and the likelihood of substantial error, it may be prudent to round to the nearest million rather than to the nearest thousand. Researchers must make that decision for themselves for every data set they use. Awareness of sampling or selection error is more important than the precise size of the correction because it alerts readers to the presence of possible unspecified error. (For a more detailed discussion of sampling designs and sampling error, see Kalton [1983].)

2. MEASUREMENT ERRORS AND INVALIDITY

Sampling and selection errors are only one source of inaccuracy in published data; in many instances, they are not the most significant source of error. A second deficiency that generally affects published data is measurement error. Measurement error takes many forms. Some errors arise from mistakes in conceptualization; others flow from structural characteristics of the data collection process. Let us first turn to errors stemming from conceptual problems. These may be particularly acute for users of published data because they have little control over the ways in which concepts have been operationalized. Users of published data are prisoners of decisions about conceptualization made by those who originally collected the data.

Conceptualization Errors and Construct Validity

Differences in meaning between concepts and indicators are the cause of many errors in interpreting analyses using published data. All empirical research moves from abstract concepts to concrete measures. Researchers must concern themselves both with a careful specification of their concepts and a faithful operationalization of those concepts in concrete terms.

Concepts themselves posit some "true" value for a variable. For instance, the concept of "cost of living" presumes that one can imagine some number that truly represents how much it costs to live in a middle-class style or some other style in the United States. "Literacy" posits a measurement of the ability to read and write at a specified level. "Budget deficit" infers an excess of spending over revenues. Every question that a social scientist wishes to research is defined by such a set of concepts. A political scientist may wish to examine the ways in which "politics" affects the "outputs" of "government." A criminologist may concern herself with the "sources" of "criminal behavior." A sociologist may focus on "family structure." An economist may wish to analyze the concomitants of "unemployment." Each of these concepts has many commonplace meanings. Social scientists, however, usually wish to attach a very particular definition to concepts that, through a series of operations, permit them to measure their occurrence. That way of defining concepts is called operationalization.

In operationalizing concepts, one always must substitute concrete indicators for the abstract, true value of the concept. Those indicators may miss the mark because they lack validity or they may be faulty because of unreliability. In this section we concern ourselves only with validity.

An indicator is said to be valid when the fit between it and the underlying concept is close. Although this is an elementary rule of empirical research, it is by no means simple to observe. Concepts are abstract, while measurements of indicators are concrete. The two are rarely identical and, when not identical, the gap between them introduces error into analyses. Even with such physical concepts as "heat" the gap is considerable. Heat is measured by temperature; the temperature that must be attained to boil water or melt iron at a given altitude is well known and can be determined with minimal error. However, the associated concept, "I am hot" is far trickier. A reading of 80 degrees Fahrenheit will feel hot to one person while another will find it comfortable. For that reason weather reports often speak of such measures as a "temperature-humidity index" or a "wind chill factor." Even such measures, however, do not tap the prior experience of those who are exposed to the elements, a factor that is important because it is a commonplace observation that 40 degrees in February feels much warmer than 40 degrees in June; likewise, a 40 degree day in February in Miami is "freezing cold" while the same day in Chicago is unseasonably warm. Thus a gap remains between concept and indicator. When the concept being considered is as complex as the subjective perception of "hot" or "cold", numbers on a gauge provide only a guide; considerable error remains in applying those numbers to the concept in question. Most readers probably think that "hot" and "cold" are simple concepts. Social concepts are often considerably more complex.

A partial remedy for these problems is to follow the example of weather forecasters and utilize several measures for a concept, all the while recognizing that the fit between measure and concept will not be perfect. Take for instance the concept of "deficits" as applied to governmental finances. In everyday language, "deficit" means an excess of expenditure over revenue. Governments, however, have much more complex financial arrangements than individuals or small businesses. They have many accounts, some of which may be overdrawn while others are solvent. With the federal government, the size of the deficit is quite different if one includes all social security revenues and payments or if one treats them separately. In addition, there is a considerable difference between the amount actually paid out during any given time span and the amounts obligated but not yet paid.

Procedures for determining whether a measure is valid or not have been most fully developed by psychologists dealing with nonexperimental data (Campbell and Fisk, 1959; Campbell and Stanley, 1966; Cook and Campbell, 1979; see also Carmines and Zeller, 1979; Sullivan and Feldman, 1979). They suggest that we examine convergent and discriminant validity. A measure is valid when it converges with expectations derived from other knowledge about the subject matter or when it discriminates between different concepts. With respect to the ways in which official publications define deficits, one may ask whether those governmental units that report deficits also report borrowing funds; moreover, if they are legally prohibited from having deficits (as many state and local goverments in the United States are), we should find some indication of fiscal stress when deficits occur. If neither borrowing nor indicators of stress exist, the operationalization of the concept of "deficit" that we find in official sources needs to be questioned.

Another example of convergent validity is the measure of "communications development" in various nations. Clearly it is important for many analyses that seek to compare political processes across nations to have a rough measure of the capacity of governments and the populace to communicate with one another. Measures of newspaper circulation, of the number of radio and television sets, of mail use, and the number of telephones each represent only a portion of the concept and each are full of potential errors. However, if these measures correlate closely with one another, they can be combined into an index of communications development (cf. Taylor and Hudson, 1972: 208-209). We may have more confidence in such a combined index of convergent measures than in a single indicator.

Discriminant validity is useful in considering ways in which we might infer family size from census data. Suppose one wishes to compare the income of nuclear families with that of extended families. Unfortunately, the census counts households rather than families. The nuclear family, as used by sociologists, usually refers to a unit with a husband and/or wife with their minor children. Extended families also include stepchildren, grandparents, adult children, cousins or others who do not necessarily live together (Barber, 1953: 3-4; Cherlin, 1981: 30-31). Households, as defined by the census, include not only related persons but also people who are not related by blood or marriage but who are living together. Note that even a measure that counts people living together is not entirely clear, because some people sleep in the same place without regularly taking meals together while others regularly take meals together without sharing sleeping space. For the social scientist who wishes to use census data on households for studies in which the concept, "nuclear" or "extended" family is important, the problem is that census indicators of "households" do not discriminate among different kinds of families. Failing to make such a discrimination should alert us to a potentially invalid measurement.

Control over the validity of indicators varies with the degree to which researchers are involved in collecting their data. Where researchers can design the measures they use, they usually have considerable control over their validity. Even in such circumstances, validity remains problematic, but the researcher can devise alternative measures if her first attempt fails the test of convergent or discriminant validity. When she uses published data, however, she has almost no control over the measurements. In such a case, she must examine closely the construction of the indicators in the source she is consulting and evaluate their validity for her use.

The dilemma as well as a potential solution is illustrated by the problems confronting the political scientist wishing to examine the impact of inflation on political stability. Let us suppose that her model is one that leads her to think that perceptions of inflation will lead to political unrest. Moreover, she may have substantial reason to believe that price rises will have variable effects on different elements of the population. She might reach for the *Statistical Abstract* to examine the Consumer Price Index (CPI) as her measure of inflation. That would clearly be an error. She needs data on *perceptions* of inflation or on its incidence on different strata of the population. The CPI provides neither. However, examination of Gallup or Harris public opinion polls as well as polling data available in computer readable form from the Interuniversity Consortium for Political and Social Research at the University of Michigan might provide the perceptual data desired. The CPI, however, is inappropriate because it does not discriminate between the incidence of inflation and perceptions of inflation. Even if it shows a rise, many people may not be aware of increased prices; when it falls, other people will persist in believing that inflation is still rampant. In these situations, analysts may have no influence over the collection of the data or the construction of the measure. But they retain control over their choice of alternative data sets and continue to be free to formulate their research in a different way. However, to exercise their choices wisely, researchers must understand the ways in which the misfit between concept and measure may introduce error into their analyses.

An example of a very high degree of care in operationalizing valid indicators of important concepts in political research may be found in Kenneth Janda's *Political Parties: A Cross National Survey* (1980). Unless one defines "party" with great precision, quite different kinds of groups might be included in countries that have varying political traditions. Janda devotes many pages to specifying the several dimensions of party organization that he considers. Moreover, he provides a detailed discussion of the ways in which he utilized a wide variety of original sources in order to validate his measures. Many of his numerical indices are accompanied by an adequacy-confidence code that conveys his evaluation of the quality of the data. Users of Janda's data and others like it are in almost as good a position as the researcher who collects his data himself. The user of such data has the information needed to determine if the fit between concept and measure is a good one.

A similar set of procedures for testing validity must be used when researchers find several indicators that appear to be measuring the same concept but that have not been combined into a single index. A good example is to be found in two widely used data sets about one of American society's most puzzling problems: crime. Crime data, like most gathered by government agencies, are not collected with a specific research problem in mind. In the United States, the concepts underlying crime reports reflect the orientations of two separate collecting agencies that use two quite different operationalizations of crime. One data set is the National Crime Survey, an ongoing national survey of "victimizations" in which people are asked by the Census Bureau about incidents in which they were criminally victimized. The second comes from police reports and is published by the Federal Bureau of Investigation as the *Uniform Crime Reports.*

The National Crime Survey asks a random sample of respondents if they have been victims of a crime within the preceding six months. Like all sample surveys, it is subject to sampling error and the publications of the survey provide information for estimating the size of the error. The major problems with these crime statistics concern the ways in which the concept of crime has been operationalized (Penick and Owens, 1976; Skogan, 1981). Since several persons may be victimized in the same incident, the number of victimizations is not equivalent to the number of crimes. Moreover, collecting information from victims produces a number of peculiarities. The first is that one can measure only those crimes for which victims can be found. No murders are reported in victimization surveys, since murder victims can scarcely be interviewed. Nor does the survey report drug, prostitution, or gambling offenses, since these are typically "victimless" crimes in the sense that the "victims" are also the offenders, and they are not likely to report on themselves to a census interviewer. Another limitation is that only those victimizations that occur to persons over the age of 12 are included; no child abuse or elementary school-yard crimes are included. These and many other considerations drive a large wedge between the concept of "crime" and the measure of criminality as reflected in victimizations.

The second set of data have different but equally severe problems (Biderman and Reiss, 1967; Skogan, 1975). These data are composed of offenses known to the police (Federal Bureau of Investigation); it is not a sample but a count. This set is available annually for most cities with more than 25,000 inhabitants since the mid-1930s. Over the years, however, the components of the data set have changed, and the data have been collected with increasing accuracy. In this data set, crime has been operationalized as those offenses that the police know about and that they record as crimes. The police may reduce this measure of crime by "unfounding" reports (that is, reclassifying them as noncrimes), by failing to record incidents, or by not responding to citizen calls about crimes. Moreover, the measure is sensitive to the willingness of citizens to call the police in the first place. If people decide that it is not worth their time to call the police after having been victimized, the incident will never be recorded as a crime. Thus this second data set is quite sensitive to variations in citizen reporting and bureaucratic recording.

Neither measure is a valid indicator of the sum total of all criminal activity in the United States. Just as several important categories of crimes remain unreported in victimization surveys, many crimes are not reported to the police, and others are sometimes not recorded by them. Both data sets fail to measure incivility like graffiti on subways, petty disorders, and unruliness that make people fearful and that many would consider crimes.

Moreover, the two measures do not converge; they do not measure the same thing. During the 1970s, the National Crime Survey (U.S. Department of Justice, 1979) reported that victimizations were essentially constant, while the *Uniform Crime Reports* indicated that they were rising (U.S. Bureau of the Census, 1981: 170). Each records quite different levels of crime, with the National Crime Survey measuring a much higher level of crime (i.e., victimizations) than does the Offenses Known to the Police indicator. Finally, the two measures have been found to be related in different ways to independent variables such as population density, unemployment, and the proportion of the population that is black (Booth et al., 1977).

We can be sure that the published data do in fact reflect some proportion of what an analyst means by "crime," but it will always be a variable proportion. Therefore, someone who wishes to study crime with these data must make two crucial decisions. The first concerns the manner in which crime is to be defined. If the focus is on the police and their interaction with offenders, the Offenses Known to the Police indicator may be the most appropriate one. If the focus is closer to victims and their involvement in crimes, the National Crime Survey data are likely to be preferred. If one wishes to include incivility in the measure of crime, neither indicator will be adequate. The second decision concerns the errors embedded in each set. One must decide whether the measurement error of the indicator can be tolerated.

The decision to accept or reject such measurement errors hinges on several factors. One is the availability of alternative data that might be superior to those at hand. Where such alternative exist, they should be used if resources can be mustered to obtain them. Often, however, alternatives have unexplored measurement errors and are costly in both money and time. A second criterion is the size of differences that are likely to be found in comparing sets of data. If the differences are very large, small validity errors may not be important. A third criterion is the purpose of the analysis. An exploratory study may tolerate larger measurement errors than one that seeks to confirm or disconfirm a set of hypotheses. A study on which important public policy consequences hinge requires more caution than one that will be limited to the classroom.

Occasions will arise when it may be wiser to abandon an analysis than to conduct it with the flawed data that have been published unless one can make the necessary corrections in them. One instance for such caution is the analysis of crime across nations. The researcher not only confronts the difficulties described for American data, but he also encounters substantial variations in what is considered and counted as criminal behavior. The problem is most evident in dealing with crime in the Soviet Union. Ordinary crimes were for many years considered to be a relic of bourgeois culture that presumably had been eradicated under Bolshevik rule. Especially during the later Stalinist years, crime was considered to be an evidence of regime failure to a much larger degree than in the United States, and crime counts were considered politically sensitive. It is generally agreed among Soviet specialists that such counts were very difficult to obtain and when obtained are likely to be quite unreliable (Shelley, 1979).

Ineptitude and organizational confusion may contaminate data in the same way as ideology. Court data about the processing of criminals in the United States provides such an example. The Department of Justice has published occasional state-by-state counts and estimates of civil and criminal cases initiated in courts (e.g., U.S. Bureau of the Census, 1982-83: 189). Those data remain fragmentary despite the agency's best efforts to standardize data categories and to collect comprehensive information. The data include the unlikely report that Illinois filed 519,000 criminal cases in 1977 while in the same year California (with more than twice the population filed only 57,000 cases (U.S. Bureau of the Census, 1981: 187). Tracing those statistics back, one discovers that they refer only to the state's highest criminal court. In Illinois, all criminal cases—both felonies and misdemeanors— go to the circuit courts, although the vast majority of cases are misdemeanors. In California, the courts that reported these statistics handle only felonies. These two different ways of operationalizing "criminal cases filed" would lead the unwary observer to the mistaken conclusion that Illinois is much more active in filing criminal cases than is California. These court statistics are so blemished that it would probably be better not to use them at all unless one can certify them through independent investigations.

Measurement mistakes flowing from the invalidity of the operationalization of abstract concepts are widespread in using published data. One may be trapped not only by one's own mistakes in operationalizing indicators, but one may also be trapped by the peculiarities of the operationalizations guiding collectors of the data. One needs to be particularly sensitive to indications that measures are convergent with concepts and that they discriminate between alternative concepts. One may need to look for additional measures of what one seeks to study, or one may have to choose between alternative data sets that are readily available. In a few cases, one may need to consider collecting one's own data or to abandon the project because the measurement problems are insuperable.

Errors Produced by Changing Circumstances

Somewhat different problems arise with concepts that have changed meaning over time. A prime example of such a concept is the standard (or cost) of living. Living styles change as new goods and technologies become available. They may change in different ways for people who live in urban rather than rural areas, for farmers and for clerks. These variations require that our measures of the cost of living must have different components for different circumstances, whether they be different countries and cultures or different time periods.

One instance of such a measure in the United States is the Consumer Price Index, which is often interpreted as an indicator of inflation or the cost of living. The CPI continually suffers from the inability of a statistical measure to keep up with changes in the social and economic environment. Although designed to measure the pace of inflation, it was itself a victim of inflation during the 1970s because of the way it was for many years calculated (Blinder, 1980; Gordon, 1981; Wahl, 1982). A major component of consumer prices or cost of living is the cost of housing. For many years this element of the index reflected the most recent real estate transactions and mortgage rates, even though the housing cost of most persons who were buying their homes was frozen at the time they made their purchase. Thus, by the early 1980s when current costs soared and the mortgage rate exceeded 15%, the CPI reflected very high housing costs, although only a small portion of home owners paid those amounts, and most paid much smaller sums because they had purchased their homes at a time when prices and interest rates were lower. Housing costs (other than taxes and utilities, which were measured separately) actually remained constant for most of the population, but the cost of living index supposed and reported the opposite. Consequently, the actual rise in the cost of living experienced by many Americans during the early 1980s was lower than what was reported by the Consumer Price Index. Other changes in life-styles also have affected the CPI, with the result that it usually fails to reflect changing consumer preferences until many years after the fact. Thus, in 1977 the CPI was based on data reflecting consumer preferences sixteen years earlier; a revision of the index in that year used data that were already more than five years old (Gordon, 1981: 117). Keeping the index up to date involves problems of staggering detail. Gordon reports on it as follows:

> From 1918 to 1940, the CPI index that covered shaving was the price of a barber shave, and then switched in 1940 to the safety-razor blade, despite the fact that safety razors had largely replaced barber shaves in the 1920's. From 1940 to 1952 the index item was the blade, joined from 1952 to 1964 by shaving cream, followed from 1964 to 1977 by the shaving cream alone, followed since 1977 by a combination of dental and shaving toiletry products. Since 1964 there has been no blade in the CPI, and thus no consideration of the new world opened up for most men by the invention of the double-edged blade in the 1970's.
>
> Other products have come and gone as well. In 1940 the index dropped not only barbershop shaves, but also high button shoes, men's nightshirts, and girls' cotton bloomers. The 1953 revision eliminated salt pork and laundry soap but added televisions, frozen foods, Coca-Cola, and whiskey. Pajamas, which had replaced nightshirts in 1940, themselves disappeared in 1964, leaving only sheets and blankets to cover the sleeping American male. Appendectomies also disappeared in 1964, the year funeral services were added. Among the new product categories introduced in the 1978 revision were pet supplies and expenses, indoor sports equipment, tranquilizers, and electronic pocket calculators [Gordon, 1981: 128].

Gordon's account illustrates the difficulty of keeping up with changing life-styles. Moreover, even standardized items come in a bewildering assortment of brands and prices. No index can take that variety into account and keep pace with changing products and consumer preferences to yield a timely and affordable indicator. For some purposes, these errors may make no difference; for others they may be critical. For the political scientist who wishes to examine the effect of inflation on voters' perceptions of what issues are important in national politics, it is essential that the inflation measure reflect real rather than artifactual changes in price levels. For such an analysis, an equal measure of vigilance must be exercised with the indicator of voter perceptions. Without these precautions, the findings may simply be a product of invalid measures.

A similar difficulty accompanies cross-national comparisons of monetary sums such as governmental expenditures or consumer income. There are many problems with such comparisons, but the most obvious is the need to find a common indicator. One cannot compare dollars to marks or yen. If one converts other currencies into U.S. dollars, one must understand the distortions that are introduced by official (or unofficial) exchange rates (Taylor and Hudson, 1972: 288).

While all indices suffer from such problems to some degree, researchers who design their own index maintain some control over the dimensions of the problem. They may choose to tolerate errors of one kind while attempting to eliminate others. For instance, they might invest greater resources to make their index more accurate for urbanites while neglecting the unique problems of rural residents. Alternatively, if one were particularly concerned about the effects of unemployment on urban black youth, one would design an index that would pick up not only those youth actively looking for work (as the present unemployment indicators do) but also those discouraged from job seeking, who are excluded from the published unemployment statistics. If one were studying the effects of middle-class unemployment, one would want an index that also considered the effects of underemployment (both in time and in skills), but this is not important for studying unemployment among teenagers with few skills. Researchers using published data rarely enjoy such options. They must take indicators as they are published, even when they are inadequate for their purposes.

A related set of problems arises from shifts in the definition of indicators. Such shifts occur in a number of ways. One common problem for political scientists is that the boundaries of their units of analysis change. Students of national politics must accommodate themselves to changes in national boundaries just as researchers of city politics must deal with cities that grow by annexation. For instance, the Phoenix of 1978 bears faint resemblance to the Phoenix of 1948. During that 30-year period, the city added 265 square miles, an area larger than the city of Chicago. The population of Phoenix increased almost sevenfold from 100,000 to 690,000. By almost every measure, the unit that the analyst is studying may be different in one time period than in the other. Every measure associated with the city has a different meaning in 1978 than it had in 1948, yet it is often considered as if it were unchanged. Scholars using national boundaries face the same problem. These boundaries rarely remain the same for all countries even during as short a period as a decade.

Other units of measurement also change. One example of such a change is reported by Morgenstern, who quotes Oskar Anderson with respect to a change in the calendar:

According to the census of January 1, 1910, Bulgaria had a total of 527,311 pigs; 10 years later, according to the census of January 1, 1920, their number was already 1,089,699, more than double. But, he who would conclude that there had been a rapid development in the raising of pigs in Bulgaria (a conclusion that has indeed been drawn) would be greatly mistaken. The explanation is quite simply that in Bulgaria, almost half the number of pigs is slaughtered before Christmas. But after the war, the country adopted the "new" Gregorian calendar, abandoning the "old" Julian calendar, but it celebrates the religious holidays still according to the "old" manner, i.e. with a delay of 13 days. Hence January 1, 1910 fell after Christmas when the pigs were already slaughtered and January 1, 1920, before Christmas when the animals, already condemned to death, were still alive and therefore counted. A difference of 13 days was enough to invalidate completely the exhaustive figures [Morgenstern, 1963: 46-47].

Yet another source of this problem is a change in the application of some otherwise apparently constant rules. For instance, the concept of legal majority, when persons are held responsible for their own acts, seems on the surface to have remained relatively constant in recent times. However, the age at which young people assume the legal responsibility of adults has been changed in most places in the United States from 21 to 18 during the last 15 years, thus changing the meaning of many age categorizations. Likewise, the official definition of poverty in the United States changes with each administration; the definition of metropolitan area shifts every second or third decade.

Survey data also often present troubling challenges to researchers. Where the researcher wishes to analyze changes of public attitudes or perceptions over time, she must rely on questions in a series of surveys. In some instances, the questions will have been altered in minor or major ways from one survey to the next. Such changes make it difficult to decide whether findings are the result of real changes in attitudes or whether they are the artifact of the changes in the questions. The debate over that question is articulated well in an exchange between three sets of scholars in the *American Journal of Political Science*. Two groups (Sullivan et al., 1978; Bishop et al., 1979) asserted that the finding of greater conservatism and policy consistency among voters in the 1970s as compared with earlier voters might be the product of changes in the wording of the surveys. The third group, (Nie and Rabjohn, 1979) responded by showing that the findings were consistent with results in surveys where the questions were not changed. The exchange illustrates the care that must be exercised when using data from a series of surveys.

The problem does not always disappear when survey questions remain constant. That alone does not guarantee their validity. Social reality and popular understandings change over time; in order to capture such changed meanings, it may be necessary to alter question-naire items. Such changes confront the social researcher with a dilemma. If researchers retain constant items, their measures will increasingly depart from the social reality they are attempting to capture because that reality is continually changing. But if they alter the measure to keep up with the changing reality, they lose continuity with earlier measures. The problem has no entirely satisfactory solution. Some agencies attempt to straddle the dilemma by using both an "old" and a "new" index and devising conversion factors by which one may find equivalent values for the "old" concept using the new measure. Such conversion factors, while often the best available solution, are of dubious validity because the old indicator did not tap the phenomena measured by the new index, the reason being that these phenomena did not yet exist. Unless, by chance, one possesses measures of some underlying social phenomenon that has remained constant, one cannot validly measure social change using indicators whose definitions shift. The most promising solution is to conduct separate analyses for each portion of the time period during which the indicator remained constant. The weakness of this solution is that when one breaks a data set into several segments, one often does not have sufficient data points in each portion to conduct the type of analysis that is desired (Cook et al., 1980: 128-129).

One example of a partially successful way to address this kind of problem concerns the changing value of money. It changes in response to inflation or recession and (what Americans rarely have experienced) revaluation. Although most people think in terms of current dollars— that is, the actual number they have on their paycheck or in their bank account at any one time—economists have long converted those amounts into so-called constant dollars. Constant dollars are obtained by using a price deflator and multiplying current dollars with it. The difficulty with that procedure is that, as we have already seen with our discussion of the Consumer Price Index, such deflators themselves contain considerable error. If one wants to know how much better off one was in 1982 than in 1972, use of constant dollars is undoubtedly better than use of current dollars. However, one must be careful not to use such indicators inappropriately or to take them too literally. It may, for instance, be more valid to use current dollars when inflation is steady but slow and one wishes to make inferences about how wealthy or poor people *feel* because it is current dollars that people deal with.

Errors Arising from Inappropriate Transformations

The problem presented by the changing value of money occurs more generally. Many of the data that appear in published sources are not presented in raw form. Rather, they have been standardized by some other statistic. Just as fiscal data are often presented in constant rather than current dollars, many social statistics are the product of a transformation that involves use of another indicator. The most frequently used standard is population. Innumerable statistics are given on a per capita basis. Several errors may occur through such standardizations. Some of them arise from the use of inappropriate measures; others arise from the errors in the statistic used to make the transformation.

Mistakes are often made in choosing an appropriate measure to standardize an indicator. If one merely wishes to provide "more meaningful" comparisons, standardizing by the population is often helpful because it avoids confusing large and small effects that are simply the consequence of population size. Often, however, it is blatantly wrong to use population as a standardizer. For instance, it makes little sense to report rapes per capita when rapes are committed almost entirely against women. Yet in most of its statistical tables, the *Uniform Crime Reports* show the rape rate per 100,000 inhabitants. Moreover, it makes little sense to include young girls in the base because very few pre-adolescent girls are the victims of reported rapes. The consequence of using the inappropriate base in this instance is that rapes appear to be a much less common event than they in fact are. Education expenditures per capita also make little sense. If they are intended to show how much money was addressed to a problem, the correct measure of the "problem" is the number of school-age children, not the entire population. On the other hand, if the indicator is intended to show the resource base for such expenditures, the number of adults (excluding children) is more appropriate.

Once one becomes sensitive to this issue, one finds that a large number of indicators are calculated on the incorrect base. The correct choice is not mandated by some general rule. Rather, the base must be chosen so that it validly reflects the concept that the indicator is to measure. Inappropriate choices are sometimes made because a more appropriate base figure is unavailable or difficult to obtain. More often, standardized data are simply copied from the published source without consideration for potential misinterpretations and the availability of alternatives. Nevertheless, there may be occasions when one cannot avoid using a base that is less than optimal. When one does so, however, one should be quite conscious that the results are contaminated with the error inherent in such a choice.

In addition to the danger of choosing an inappropriate standardizer, we need to recognize the possibility that the measures used for standardization may be errorful. We have already seen how the Consumer Price Index is subject to error from many sources. We have also seen that many of the same errors and some additional ones are embedded in the population statistics from the U.S. Census (U.S. Congress, Subcommittee on Census and Population). Use of more errorful population estimates creates even more dubious statistics. Take, for example, cross-national per capita estimates. The *World Handbook* (Taylor and Hudson, 1972) reports many such statistics. For instance, it reports the number of students per one million population. For Saudi Arabia, the number is given as 240 in 1964 with no warning that this might be a biased estimate (p. 231); however, as we have seen, the editors indicate on another page (296) that the population estimate for Saudi Arabia has a 30.8% error margin. Regardless of the accuracy of the count of students (or anything else), when standardized by an errorful population estimate, the per capita statistic itself becomes contaminated with error. Whenever a measure is standardized by some other indicator, the careful researcher needs to investigate the validity and reliability of the standardizing measure. One cannot take for granted the accuracy of population statistics, monetary indices, or any of the other social indicators that are used to standardize statistics.[1]

Still another source of error in population counts and other standardizing statistics is their unavailability for the time period the researcher needs. Suppose one wishes to calculate crime rates or per capita divorce rates for cities on an annual basis. The required population statistics exist only for years in which the census was taken— for instance, 1960, 1970, and 1980 in the United States. To produce annual crime or divorce rates one needs to estimate population for each of the intervening years. That is most appropriately done when one knows the population count both for the beginning and the end of the period one is concerned with. Then one may estimate the intervening years by apportioning the change (growth or decline) to each of the nine years between censuses (Smith and Zopf, 1976; 574-579). Usually that ought not to be done by simply dividing the difference by nine; such an estimate assumes an equal growth or decline for each of the nine years, something that is quite unlikely. Rather, demographers tend to use a log-linear estimate, which has the effect of adding last year's change to the base before calculating the next data point. It assigns the largest proportion of the change to later years. Even that solution, however, still depends on uncomfortable assumptions. Without further information, one does not know whether growth occurred only during some years while during others there was a decline. One also does not know whether the growth occurred in relatively regular amounts or whether there were spurts during some years (for instance, during years of substantial economic growth) while it tapered off during other years.

Consequently, one may seek additional information about population change from such sources as utility hook-ups, health department records, or building permits. In most cases, however, few of those sources are readily available, and all are subject to their own errors. Therefore, researchers face the unenviable choice of selecting an inappropriate measure (for instance, one that is badly outdated) or using one that is full of unknown errors. It is a decision that is routinely made, but often the choice is exercised without an awareness of the possible extent to which an analysis may be damaged by it. In order to avoid misleading readers by inappropriate confidence in one's data, researchers are obligated to report their awareness of validity problems with their data and to indicate the consequences those problems pose for the researcher's conclusions.

Another danger lurks in the use of errorful standardizers (Schuessler, 1974; Fuguitt and Lieberson, 1974; Uslaner, 1976; Long, 1980). When one uses standardized indicators in multivariate analyses, the errors in the standardizer will obviously introduce unknown error into the analysis. That error cannot be estimated by referring to standard estimates of error that such analyses routinely produce, because those estimates of error refer to simple sampling error in the variables and not to the compounded error produced when two indicators are multiplied or divided by one another. In addition, one needs to take care not to include the same variable on both sides of the equation as the result of standardizing variables in terms of rates; that produces some degree of spuriousness in the analysis. For instance, one should not rely on the correlation coefficients between crime rate and per capita income because some of the relationship is produced by the population element that is common to both indicators. The recommended solution is to leave the dependent variable (the crime count in the example above) in its raw form and use the standardizing variable (for example, population) as one of the independent variables. Such procedures avoid the error of spurious correlation although they do nothing to reduce the errors that are inherent in the standardizing indicators.

Summary

Challenges to validity of measures are a fundamental problem that researchers using published data must address. Concepts that interest the researcher are often not those motivating those who collect data or who devise measures for public agencies. Challenges to validity arise from the inability of researchers who use published data to design their own indicators and the consequent gap between concept and indicator. Other problems arise from changes in concepts that may be inadequately reflected by published indicators. Still other problems come from the use of inappropriate indicators for standardizing measures. Sensitivity to these problems is the first requirement for sensible use of such data. Such sensitivity alerts the researcher to look for analysis errors that are the consequence of a mismatch between concepts and data. When compromises must be made, as is often the case, they should also be reported.

3. RELIABILITY

Reliability is the third major concern of empirical researchers. Reliability refers to the ability to obtain consistent results in successive Reliability refers to the ability to obtain consistent results in successive measurements of the same phenomenon. A scale is considered reliable if it records the same number each time a five-pound weight is placed on it. A count of the number of schools is reliable if successive counts (for the same date) produce identical results.

Reliability does not come cheaply. Consider, for instance, forecasting the size of the Florida orange crop. A reliable forecast depends on many factors; fundamental to all is knowledge of the condition of the crop. According to the *Wall Street Journal* [September 14, 1983: 1], sixty men were employed in 1983 to climb 4500 trees. Their job was to count the number of oranges on the tree limbs. Tree limbs were selected randomly, and the men climbed up them to count the oranges. The oranges on each limb were counted by two different men; if their count was not the same, they were told to recount. If they still did not agree, the supervisor climbed up and his count became the official one. One wonders, of course, what happens when no reporter is watching. Sometimes counts are faked in such operations. If every published statistic were collected with the care exhibited by the orange counters, reliability would be a smaller problem.

The user of published data cannot take it for granted that care has been exercised in the collection and reporting of information. A colleague tells a story of how a count of date trees was conducted in a village of a Third World country. An official from the central agriculture ministry arrived at the village and asked the village elder how many date trees were in the village. The elder replied, "Who knows?" After several exchanges of this sort, the elder finally exploded with impatience and told the official to write down "sixty." And sixty it became in the official statistics. Such problems, however, are not limited to Third World data. Suppose, for instance, that you were interested in analyzing gender gap in voter turnout in the United States. A number of different studies report voter turnout by sex. Table 1 shows the data from four studies for the year 1968. All four claim to be relying on the same data source—the sample surveys of the Survey Research Center at the University of Michigan—yet none of the four studies agrees with any of the others. For other years, the estimates are sometimes closer and sometimes farther apart. The analyst's conclusions appear to hinge on whether the data were taken from an earlier or later data tape, or from a published report of the data. Such mutations of data from an apparent common source often result from successive handling by archival employees and analysts.[2]

Reliability is very much a function of the characteristics of the organizations that produce and publish the data. All data are collected by organizations, large or small. Even the individual researcher often relies on assistants to photocopy or hand copy data from published sources. Such assistants are likely to make mistakes as the orange counters do, and the researcher must take the same precautions to check his assistant's accuracy. The problems increase exponentially when one depends on other organizations for one's data collection, because the

TABLE 1
Voting Turnout by Sex in 1968 in the United States (percentages)

Source	Men	Women
Lansing (1974: 8)	76	73
Lynn (1979: 406)	69	66
Poole and Zeigler (1982: Table 2)	77	72.4
Miller et al. (1980: 317)	78.1	74.1

researcher has no influence on the organizational procedures that produce his data. The more one relies on published data, the more one needs to know the organizational quirks that governed the collection and archiving of the materials.

Clerical Errors

Simple clerical errors are the bane of every research endeavor. Every research organization must make some attempt to identify their source and to minimize their effect. The usual measures include screening personnel so that the careless are given other work or are not hired at all. Those assigned to work with data must be trained so that they carry out their tasks correctly. Someone must check the data for accuracy. This may include repunching the data (using a verifier) and comparing the collected data with some other set. Incentives must exist for accurate work. No data that have not been subjected to such checks warrant our trust.

Yet some important data sets are routinely used even though they have not been subject to such precautions. The most prominent of these are election returns. Ballots are counted in tens of thousands of precincts across the country. Some of them are printed ballots on which voters indicated their choice with pen or pencil; these need to be counted manually. Others are cast on machines that automatically tally the results; still others are cast on punch cards which must be run through a counting machine. After the count has been determined, it must be recorded, telephoned to a central office where the results again must be copied, tallied, and recorded.

The employees who perform these tasks in the United States are barely trained part-timers. They are recruited by party organizations mostly for individual elections. They work a single long day from early in the morning when the polls open until the ballots have been counted in the evening. At best, most receive a few hours of training before election day, but many are doing it for the first (and last) time because counting ballots is not a task that is routinely and repetitively performed. Thus it is little wonder that results are not accurate to the last ballot even in honest elections, and we know that not all elections in our past have been honest. In most elections, counting errors make no difference in the outcome since the margin of victory is more than five percentage points and the error is probably less. But when a race is especially close, the winner is probably determined by error. For instance, in the 1982 Illinois gubernatorial contest, the margin between the incumbent James Thompson and his Democratic challenger, Adlai Stevenson III, was only 5,000 votes out of 3,6000,000 ballots. Because this is a population count rather than a random sample, we cannot precisely estimate the margin of error, but it seems likely that the official margin, which was less than two-tenths of one percent, was well within the boundaries of such an error. Assume no systematic error (such as ballot theft) in the original count; if 100 recounts were taken, one would expect Thompson to win about 50 and Stevenson to win the other 50. In such close elections, one cannot determine the winner with any confidence; one can only surmise that the race was a virtual tie.

How should researchers treat election results and similar counts when doing research? Some caution is certainly in order. When using raw totals for large jurisdictions, it is absurd to believe that the count is accurate to more than the closest thousand. In other words, one would be well advised to disregard the last three (or perhaps even four) digits of the official count. In elections and in many other instances, the official count is required by law to report the returns down to the last item. To do otherwise in elections would imply that individual votes didn't matter because they were not counted; moreover, a winner has to be designated. Consequently, voting statistics are often published, as in *America Votes* (Scammon et al., annual), with excessive pseudo-accuracy. Researchers, knowing that errors are inevitable in the counting process, should treat the count in rounded-off thousands or ten thousands.

Searching for such counting errors and the other reliability problems we will discuss below must have a high priority for all users of published statistics. Several procedures are available. Whether one has cross-sectional data (many observations at one point in time) or longitudinal data, one needs to display them in a scatter plot. Such a plot will reveal whether any cases are so deviant from the mean or the regression line that they require further investigation. Moreover, one can compare the display of one set of data with other sets that, according to one's knowledge of the phenomena, should look similar. If they do not, they bear further investigation. For instance, the data on per capita newspaper circulation in the *World Handbooks* appear suspect when one compares the numbers from the first two editions. For the United States, the per capita figures for 1960 are 326 and for 1965, 310 (Russett et al., 1964: 108; Taylor and Hudson, 1972: 242). The drop in per capita newspaper circulation seems correct if one compares it with the rise in television sets and assumes that people are substituting television for newspapers. However, if one then looks at Sweden, one finds the reported per capita newspaper circulation rose between 1960 and 1965, while the number of television sets increased even more than in the United States. Either the Swedes did not substitute television for newspapers or the data for the United States or Sweden are incorrect. On the surface, at least, such a comparison casts doubts on the reliability of the reported data. Without comparing the data from several years, one is likely to accept the numbers from one volume or the other uncritically because the tables themselves give the reader no reason to exercise exceptional caution. The comparison forces the researcher to examine the data more closely.

Changes in Collection Procedures

Official statistics often change in subtle ways that reflect changes in the organizations that collect them. The headings in official tables remain the same even though the numbers mean something slightly different because of the way in which they were collected. One needs to search for such organizational changes and take them into account when using the data that organizations produce. Again, we may use voting statistics as an example. Registration statistics may reflect not only changes in the number of persons registering but also changes in registration requirements such as the decline in use of literacy tests and the reduction in the voting age. Other changes may be more subtle, such as alterations in the ballot-counting process that took place in the 1960s and 1970s. Paper ballots were disappearing while some form of machine readable ballot or voting machine came into increasing use. Consequently, the error discount that we attach to the vote count ought probably to be higher for election results preceding 1960 than for more recent ones. One must exercise similar caution in interpreting statistics on the incidence of particular diseases, because they reflect not only the actual incidence of those illnesses but also variations in the health agency's ability to detect them. As medical knowledge and instrumentation improve, more illnesses can be identified and reported.

Corrections Made by Collection Agency

Data are sometimes inconsistent from one report to the next because they have been subjected to an internal review and correction process. Thus, the numbers reported for a given year change from one volume to another of a statistical report. These changes reflect corrections for errors of which the agency has become aware. Sometime these corrections are simply for printing errors. Often, however, the alterations reflect an ongoing or periodical cleansing process. Some agencies inspect their data and issue corrections when they feel it is necessary. Researchers need to be aware of this correction process for several reasons. First, if they wish to use data with the least number of clerical errors, they need to know what cleansing process the organization used and the publication schedule for the corrected information. Second, if researchers are constructing a time series, they need to be aware that the earliest points of their series may be composed of corrected data while more recent points in their series may be uncorrected or partially corrected. Greater errors may be contained in the latter than in the former.

Many of the most frequently used economic indicators are treated in this way, and the differences between early estimates and "final" statistics may be quite substantial. An example is the gross national product (GNP), one of the most frequently used economic indicators.

TABLE 2

The 1976 Gross National Product as Reported in Five Successive
Volume of *Statistical Abstract of the United States*

Year	Billions of Dollars
1977	1691.6
1978	1706.5
1979	1700.1
1980	1702.2
1981	1718.0

SOURCES: U.S. Bureau of the Census, **Statistical Abstract of the United States**
(1977: 428; 1978: 440; 1979: 435; 1980: 437; 1981: 420).

Table 2 shows the United States' GNP for 1976 from five recent
Statistical Abstracts. The difference between the 1977 and 1981 reports
is $26.4 billion or 1.5%. It is particularly large between 1980 and 1981
because in 1981 a substantial correction was made that affected many of
the previous years. Such large corrections are more often made during
the first one or two years after a statistic is published than later. In the
GNP series, the correction between first publication and the second year
often exceeds $2 billion.

The propensity of agencies to correct their data poses special
problems for the researchers who collect their data at one time and then
use it several years later. Unless they update their data in the same way as
the agency does, their published findings may be at variance with other
analyses that use the newer versions of the data.

As with the vote count, there is a tendency to publish economic
statistics with exaggerated accuracy even when no legal or ritualistic
reason exists (as it does with the vote count) to justify it. Notice that the
data in Table 2 are published to the nearest $100 million. Both public
and private organizations often publish data to the nearest one or two
decimal places, although the error inherent in those data are 10 or 100
times greater than that. In the case of GNP data, little would be lost if we
rounded to the nearest billion or even nearest 10 billion. Such rounding
signals the user that the data are not accurate to the last integer, not to

speak of the last decimal place. It prevents the analyst and reader from assuming greater precision than in fact exists.

Manipulation of Data

Another set of problems arises from the contamination of data by ideological or organizational values. The data that organizations collect can have favorable or unfavorable consequences for them; sometimes organizations try to tilt the data collection process in their favor. An illuminating although fictional example was given by Alexander Solzhenitsyn in his novel, *Cancer Ward* (1969). The hospital in which much of the action takes place managed to keep its mortality rate low by discharging terminally ill patients several days before their death. When the patients died, they died at home and were not counted among those dying while under the hospital's care.

It is difficult to know how widespread such practices are, but we can be certain that they occur. In an American state mental institution, for instance, a worker reported two major changes in its apparent workload that reflected budgetary constraints rather than changes in either the population the hospital served or in the characteristics of its patients. The first change was that between 1981 and 1982 the number of violent juveniles sent to it plummeted. However, that did not reflect a decline in youthful violence. Rather, whereas in 1981 violent youths were sent to the mental hospital, in 1982 they were handled by the criminal justice system and sent to jail.

The second change was the number of patients with suicidal tendencies declined according to official records. This decline, however, did not reflect a drop in patients with suicidal tendencies, but rather resulted from a change in record keeping. Because the institution's budget had been cut and it was short-staffed, its doctors were loathe to categorize patients as suicidal since that would require the hospital to provide closer supervision for them. The hospital no longer had the staff to provide such care. Yet, if such supervision were not given to patients recorded as suicidal, the institution might be sued for medical malpractice. Hence the solution was to alter the records and report fewer patients with suicidal tendencies.[3]

Another example is the well-known tendency for schools to prep their pupils just before giving them standardized tests on which their success in educating children will be judged. The test scores may therefore not tap general knowledge of a subject but only reflect the degree to which pupils remembered answers to particular questions that they had been given earlier. Parents are also familiar with the juggling that accompanies the number of days that children are officially in school. Children are sometimes kept in school in the morning just long enough for the day to count before being sent home either because of a snow storm or because in-service training or conferences are to take place. It is important to the school to have the day recorded as a school day in the official attendance count because the size of the school's state grant often depends on the number of days it is officially in session.

Legislative roll calls produce false statistics for still another reason. Adoption of legislation involves many votes. Some are on procedural issues; others are on amendments; finally, the bill as completed must be voted upon. These votes have varying significance. Sometimes the crucial vote comes on a procedural issue; at other times one or another amendment would have the effect of gutting the bill or changing it substantially, and the vote on that amendment is the crucial one. The final vote often, but not always, has the least significance. The *Congressional Record* and the journals of many other legislative bodies record roll call votes without weighting their significance. Consequently, all serious students of legislative roll calls must make their own assessment of the votes and weight them accordingly. Simple indices based on all votes or on all final votes will necessarily be quite misleading because the votes do not mean what they appear to mean.

Data do not only mirror internal characteristics of the organizations collecting them; they also reflect the organization's ability to withstand external pressures. Even such a well-respected agency as the Bureau of Labor Statistics is subjected to enormous pressure to juggle its statistics. Our earlier discussion of the Consumer Price Index may have led an unwary reader to think that treating housing costs was simply a technical matter. In fact, it was a very political one, because the outcome had important consequences for all those people whose wages and pensions were linked to the index. The current housing cost exaggerated inflation, and many persons favored retaining it as a component of the index because it kept their payments ahead of real inflation. Moreover, many government agencies simply do not publish data that might be damaging to them (Gordon and Heinz, 1973). While "freedom of information" requests may pry such data from agencies, it is a difficult and time-consuming process that is beyond the financial reach of many researchers. Often government data are even beyond the reach of freedom of information requests, or the very nature of the activity may lead to the generation of false statistics. One example is the expenditure level for government intelligence activities. Such activities are usually disguised in a variety of ways. The published budget of the Central Intelligence Agency in the United States and parallel agencies elsewhere includes only a portion of the funds used for intelligence gathering. Other intelligence activities are scattered among the budgets of many other agencies. An analyst cannot discover how much money is spent on intelligence activities either for the United States or for any other country.

There are many other occasions for dissembling, and they affect sample surveys as well as data collected by other methods. For instance, it is well known that respondents in sample surveys may be reluctant to reveal information that they consider sensitive (Bradburn et al., 1979: 64-106). In some contexts that involves revealing their age; in others, it means that they will not provide accurate income data; they often will not give information about activities that are considered illicit. Thus, income data that come from sample surveys may be inaccurate; age distributions may be distorted; and information about drug use and handgun ownership may be quite misleading. Those conducting sample surveys are generally sensitive to these problems because they specialize in survey design. Secondary users who see the results of the surveys in some publication are much less likely to be aware of their limitations.

Government statistics are not the only ones subject to manipulation and misinterpretation. For instance, one cannot take at face value many of the balance sheets of private corporations, because they treat some important assets and liabilities in quite variable and arbitrary ways. Procter and Gamble, for instance, routinely has included "goodwill" among its current assets; in 1982 its annual report listed "goodwill and other assets" as being worth $440 million. Lockheed Corporation, on the other hand, did not list one penny for goodwill. Clearly such entries on the balance sheets are arbitrary estimates of assets that are extremely difficult to evaluate. Their presence on some balance sheets and absence on others represents quite different ways of handling important financial information. Similarly, seemingly technical accounting decisions to use LIFO (last-in, first-out) instead of FIFO (first-in, first-out) to determine the cost of inventory can dramatically change a corporation's balance sheet. Occasionally, one even reads of corporate officers pushing one quarter's sales back into a previous quarter in order to improve their record and enhance their chances for promotion or to increase their bonus.

Instrumentation

All data are the consequence of one person asking questions of someone else. There is a large body of literature on the art of asking questions productively in the context of a sample survey (Cannell and Kahn, 1968; Bradburn et al., 1979). Every manual will tell the neophyte that questions must be worded clearly, that they must ask for only one bit of information at a time, and that they should avoid a format that might lead to an acquiescence response set or one that might lead to respondent fatigue. To determine whether such problems existed for a particular data set, investigators should ferret out the particular questions used to elicit the information being analyzed. Sometimes it is possible to obtain copies of the entire survey instrument. That information is essential to the secondary users' ability to evaluate the reliability of the information they wished to use.

Although it is rarely acknowledged, the same strictures apply to other forms of information that are found in published sources. They are also the result of someone's asking questions. The way in which those questions are posed affects the reliability of the responses. Much statistical information is collected by forms that are routinely filled out by those in possession of the information. The categories in which the information is to be recorded must be meaningful to the persons filling out the data form. The respondents must be completely clear about the meaning of such terms as "operating" expenditures as opposed to "capital" expenditures, or cases "filed" as against cases "closed." If the forms are confusing or tiresome, the information that is recorded will be full of indeterminate errors. Some agencies are reputed to be quite careful about such matters. The U.S. Census Bureau in collecting expenditure information from local governments, for instance, sometimes sends its own workers into the field to check the accuracy of the recorded information or will make telephone calls to clarify apparent inconsistencies or ambiguities in responses. It behooves researchers using such data to examine the data collection sheets and to learn what checking procedures the collecting agency performed before embarking on their own analysis of data. Often such inquiries require a telephone call or letter to the collecting agency. Without such checking, researchers run the danger of anchoring their conclusions on differences in the data that reflect reliability errors rather than true differences in the phenomena that they are examining.

Categorization

All data must be classified in some manner. It is impossible to publish everyone's income in the census or to reproduce the full detail of every government agency's budget. The categories that are chosen, however, often introduce errors quite apart from the approximations that they represent because they may not be consistent from one year to the next or may differ in various data sources. Take, for instance, expenditures for police services. In some places in the United States, all urban police services are provided by the city police department. Its expenditures are synonymous with police expenditures. Other places, however, have police forces that operate outside the jurisdiction of the police department. The transit system may have its own police force and so may the housing authority. The parks may have another police force. However, these police expenditures are likely to be buried in the operating budgets of the transit, housing, and park agencies. Whereas in one city police expenditures include 99% of all policing activities, in another they may include only two-thirds.

That difficulty exists with many data categories. Money income by household status reported from census sample surveys depends on the surveyors' correctly categorizing the household from which they are obtaining information; it also depends on the respondents' correctly understanding the categories they are being asked about. Whether a household is composed of related or unrelated individuals is not easily, quickly, or consistently discernible. One finds the same kind of problem with obtaining information about the number of motor vehicle accidents. For instance, the U.S. Census Bureau (1982-83: 615-616) reports different data for the number of deaths from motor vehicle accidents in two adjacent tables. In one table the data are categorized by the date of the accident; in the other, they are categorized by the year of the death. Moreover, the deaths are classified by the state in which they occurred rather than the state in which the victim lived. Those classification decisions may make no difference for some analyses, but for others they will be crucial.

Summary

I have pointed to five factors that require particular attention. The first is the amount of training and supervision provided those who collect the data. The less it is, the greater the error that will have to be discounted. The second element that needs to be discovered is the internal purposes served by the data and the internal implications of statistics for an organization. Third, one needs to be concerned with potential instrumentation problems. Fourth, if researchers use data collected repeatedly over some period of time, they need to determine what changes took place in the training and supervision of the persons who collected the data they are using. The data are likely to be more accurate for some periods than for others; alternatively, the error will be in one direction during one period and in the opposite direction during another period. Fifth, researchers need to be aware of the implications of classification decisions made by the original collectors of the data.

4. CONCLUSION

The problems that accompany the use of published data are manifold, but so are the solutions. Both demand careful examination.

Perhaps the most important attribute for the user of published data is a large dose of skepticism. Whether data are found in libraries or data archives, they should not be viewed simply as providing grand opportunities for cheap analyses; they should be seen as problematic. In every case the analyst should ask, Are these data valid? In what ways might they have been contaminated so that they are unreliable? In many instances the data will pass muster. However, in many other cases the data will be revealed as flawed in some fundamental way. It is the duty of the analyst to discover the flaws and, if possible, to correct them.

Researchers must subject published data to as many tests as they can devise. They must look for convergent and discriminant validity. They must display them on scatter plots to identify suspicious deviant data points. When they find them lacking, they must devise remedial strategies. In many cases one can improve validity and reliability by joining the data with other bits of information. One can go beyond the published source to persons in the agency to learn what might be done to improve data quality. When it is not possible to improve it, one can use them with extra precautions employing such measures as avoiding exaggerated precision, alerting readers to data quality problems, and erring on the side of conservatism in interpreting one's results. In a few instances the contaminations are irremediable and the task must be abandoned.

In the preceding pages I have described many of the most common problems encountered in using published data and some of some ways of overcoming them. I summarize them in Table 3.

Most of the remedies have been sufficiently illustrated in the preceding pages; a few, however, need further elaboration. One of those is among the simplest available to the analyst: directly requesting further information about published data from the collecting agency. Two steps are required in most instances. The first is a series of telephone calls to determine who in the agency possesses the technical information that is required. This may be necessary even if the data come from a reputable archive like the Inter-University Consortium of Political and Social Research. Errors may have been introduced during the archival process; often they can be traced only by comparing the data obtained from the archive with the original data from its collector. A preliminary conversation with that person is often helpful. Such a conversation, however, must often be followed by a letter specifying the information that is needed. Correspondence is important because oral requests are often poorly formulated, misunderstood, and mislaid. In many instances, requests for technical information will receive quick and thorough attention.

TABLE 3
Summary of Data Problems and Potential Solutions

Problem	Solution
Selection Error	For random samples, specify sampling error. For counts and nonrandom samples, round off to signal error and avoid exaggerated accuracy.
Invalidity	
Construct validity: Misfit between collector's and user's conceptualization	To diagnose, look for convergence with other measures and/or ability to discriminate from other concepts. Then use multiple measures, choose most appropriate alternative measure, or abandon study if no valid measure exists.
Changing circumstances causes invalidity	Search for and use indicator underlying variable common to past and present phenomenon. Calculate "conversion" factor from old to new. Undertake separate analyses for time periods when definition remained constant.
Inappropriate transformations	Use correct variable for transforming data. Watch for errors in variable used for making the transformation. Take into account potential invalidity of transforming variable. Avoid using same transformation for both dependent and independent variables.
Unavailability of data for required data points	Interpolate using log-linear methods, supplemented by additional data.
Reliability	
Clerical errors	Look for deviant cases in scatterplot. Check amount of training given by collecting agencies. Round off.
Change in collection procedures	Make separate reliability assessments for each segment of the data.

(continued)

TABLE 3 (Continued)

Problem	Solution
Corrections made by collection agency	Look for accounts of correction procedures and the times when they were applied.
Manipulation of data	Look for media and congressional accounts of such manipulations. Talk to insiders.
Instrumentation	Search for copy of data collection instrument and examine it for instrumentation errors.
Categorization	Look for inconsistencies across place and time. Try to recombine data into more consistent categories

Scatterplots have widespread use in identifying potential trouble in a data set. They should be routinely employed during the first examination of a set of data. One should look for two warning signals. The first is deviant points that cannot be readily explained by the theory one is testing. Such deviant points do not invariably represent data errors, but often they do. One can save many hours of work and much embarrassment by searching for the errors before elaborating some new theoretical statement to account for the deviant data. One method for examining these deviant points further is to collect additional information. If the points are in a cross-sectional data set, one should look at a time series for the questionable points. For example, if Philadelphia crime statistics look suspiciously low when compared to other cities of similar size, one should examine them for a number of years before and after the original point. If the point that one originally examined does not stick out suspiciously in the time series, one can be a little more certain that the observation is not a reflection of random error. It may, of course, reflect systematically different ways of counting the data in that jurisdiction. On the other hand, if the data point is also deviant in the time series, one may find the explanation by examining the data collection methods that produced that observation. It may reflect an error or it may represent some unusual occurence.

The second test one should apply to scatter plots is whether they show much *less* variability than one would otherwise expect. A completely flat line in one time series when many others show considerable variation should lead the researcher to suspect that something may be amiss. Once more, further examination is required.

Careful examination of published data can save one from absurd results. A dramatic example comes from the work of Coale and Stephan (1962: 338) on census data that seemed to show a surprising number of teenage widowers:

> The number [of teenage widowers] listed by the Census . . . were 1,670 at age 14; 1,475 at age 15; 1,175 at 16. . . . Not until age 22 did the listed number of widowers surpass those at 14. Male divorces also decrease in number as age increases from 1,320 at age 14 to 575 at age 17.

The explanation for this curious set of numbers was that some keypunch operators moved the data one column to the right so that middle-aged males became teenagers in the census reports. In this instance Coale and Stephan simply used their prior knowledge of American culture to identify potentially incorrect data. They could not be certain that teenage widowers did not exist in the numbers originally reported by the census, but it seemed quite unlikely. Others need to follow their example. Researchers should not be afraid to apply their knowledge. As they become more familiar with their research problem, they will become more adept in identifying potential data errors.

When possible, the incorrect data should be replaced with correct information or deleted from the analysis. In some instances, however, the researcher will remain uncertain about the reliability of the data. It may look suspicious, but no definite errors can be identified. In a time series, a partial remedy may be to average observations over several time points. One may replace the original data with a rolling three- or five-year average. That has the effect of dampening the series and possibly obscuring relationships. On the other hand, if the variations reflect suspected data collection errors rather than real fluctuations, the dampening produced by the use of a rolling average is a conservative approach that avoids unwarranted findings.

Equal skepticism should be applied to cross-sectional data. Most analysts using cross-sectional indicators display little sensitivity to the effects of their choice of date at which they conduct their analysis. Many analyses use data at census years because much demographic information is available only at such time points. Other data, however, that are part of such an analysis may be drawn from continuous time series. Researchers often take those data without examining whether they are suspicious blips of a time series that indicate probable error. To do so requires some additional labor. As we have already suggested, for each suspicious cross-sectional data point, a time series of 15-20 observations should be examined to determine that the observation is not a substantially deviant case that in all likelihood reflects error rather than true variation. Only then can one proceed to the planned analysis with some confidence that the data represent relatively error-free observations.

Finally, the question of rounding data from census count or nonrandom samples will often appear troublesome because no hard rule can be recommended that will yield the exact amount of rounding to apply. Once again, researchers must depend on their knowledge of the data. If the organization that collected the data has a good reputation for collecting information carefully, a smaller rounding may be applied than when one knows that the organization is usually careless. For instance, census population counts in the United States are probably more accurate than vote counts or police crime counts. That is true because we know that census employees are trained and supervised more painstakingly than are persons who count votes or police officers who record crimes. Moreover, one has to look at the size of the statistics. Rounding three digits off numbers that are originally in the thousands is a very large correction. Reporting figures that originally are in the billions with the last three digits omitted is a much smaller correction. One must use one's best judgment in making such corrections. However, it is usually better to err in employing some degree of rounding than not to round off at all, because the rounding (whatever it is) will alert readers to data problems that might otherwise go unnoticed.

Many problems lurk among the multitude of published statistics that await researchers in their libraries. They constitute a rich lode of materials on which many substantial analyses can be performed, but these data must be refined and treated with respect. They cannot be plucked mechanically from their source and entered into an analysis. Without exception, all published statistics should be treated with suspicion. One needs to inspect them for inconsistencies and errors in reporting. One must learn about the organizations that produced them and the errors organizational preferences introduced into them. One must question the ways in which indicators were standardized. In the end, some validity and reliability problems are likely to remain unresolved, but they need never lie unaddressed in the interpretation of results.

APPENDIX: A BRIEF NOTE ON SOURCES
AND CRITIQUES OF IMPORTANT DATA SETS

A brief description of many of the most important publicly available data sets may be found in Taeuber and Rockwell (1982). The data described in that paper are all available in machine readable form; many of them are also available in published form.

The census is the richest data base on the characteristics of people in the United States. Prior to the 1980 census, most of the data were published in printed form. Much of the 1980 data are available only in microfiche or machine readable form. The Census Bureau also publishes technical reports that provide a wealth of information about particular data problems and the solutions the Census Bureau has adopted. In addition, several congressional hearings provide much information about undercounts and biases in the 1970 and 1980 censuses (see the House Subcommittee on Census and Population [U.S. Congress, 1977]; House Subcommittee on Census and Population [U.S. Congress, 1980]; Senate Committee on Governmental Affairs [U.S. Congress, 1980]).

The census is also the source of most statistics on government expenditures. Anton et al. (1980) provide a detailed and sometimes devastating critique of these numbers. Other useful critiques include Collins (1982) and Fossett and Kramer (1981).

The Consumer Price Index is a product of the Bureau of Labor Statistics. Particularly helpful critiques may be found in Blinder (1980), Gordon (1981), and Wahl (1982). Unemployment statistics are also produced by the Bureau of Labor Statistics. Some of the problems associated with these data are discussed by Shiskin (1976), Groth (1982), and statements by Norwood and Landrieu before the House Subcommitte on State, Justice and Commerce (U.S. Congress, 1976).

Economic statistics are the subject of the landmark book by Oskar Morgenstern (1963). Another more recent but more limited discussion is to be found in Parker (1982).

Crime data are cirtiqued by almost every author using them. Some of the best discussions are by Penick and Owens (1976), Skogan (1975, 1981), and Biderman and Reiss (1967).

The problems associated with vote counts have not been discussed in the literature. There are, however, some good discussions of the effects of varying registration procedures on voter turnout. For these, see Kelly et al. (1967), Kim et al. (1975), and Rosenstone and Wolfinger (1978). The counts themselves are most fully reported in Scammon et al. (annual).

The principal depository for social data is the Inter-University consortium for Political and Social Research at the University of Michigan. Its holdings include the data base for many government studies, census data, and the data files from many individual researchers and social science organizations. It also has the polling data for the Survey Research Center's election studies. Its data holdings are in machine readable form and are accompanied by considerable documentation that alerts users to potential sources of error. Other public opinion polling data are held by the National Opinion Research Center at the University of Chicago, the Roper Center at the University of Connecticut, the Institute for Research in Social Science at the University of North Carolina, and the Gallup Social Science Research Group at Princeton, New Jersey. Many smaller and specialized archives exist on other university campuses.

Cross-national data are available from a variety of United Nations publications. These are combined with data from other sources in the two editions of the *World Handbook of Political and Social Indicators*. The first (Russett et al., 1964) includes data up to 1961; the second (Taylor and Hudson, 1972) includes data through 1965. A third edition is available in machine readable form from the Inter-University Consortium for Political and Social Research and has data pertaining to the 1970s. As I indicated in the text, these data must be used with extreme caution; in many instances these volumes provide insufficient warnings about the quality of the data. A model of care for data quality is represented by Janda's *Political Parties* (1980). It provides information about political parties in 53 countries between 1950 and 1962, with further information about the history of these parties through 1978. That publication includes comprehensive information about the reliability of the reported data and the methods used to determine validity and reliability.

NOTES

1. Note, however, that when one compares two measures that are standardized with the same statistic (e.g., population size), the error introduced by that standardization is constant. In other words, one does not increase the error by using such a standardization measure.

2. I am indebted to Virginia Gray for calling my attention to these data and to the discrepancies shown in Table 1.

3. These observations were reported via personal communication with a staff member at the institution.

REFERENCES

ANTON, T. J., J. P. CAWLEY, and K. L. KRAMER (1980) Moving Money. Cambridge, MA: Oelgeschlager, Gunn & Hain.

BARBER, R. E. (1953) Marriage and Family. New York: McGraw-Hill.

BIDERMAN, A. D. and A. J. REISS, Jr. (1967) "On exploring the 'dark figure' of crime." The Annals of the American Academy of Political and Social Science (November): 1-15.

BISHOP, G. F., A. J. TUCHFARBER, and R. W. OLDENICK (1978) "Change in the structure of American political attitudes." American Journal of Political Science 22: 250-269.

————and S. E. BENNETT (1979) "Questions about question wording: a rejoinder to revisiting mass belief systems revisited." American Journal of Political Science 23: 187-192.

BLINDER, A. S. (1980) "Consumer Price Index and the measurement of recent inflation." Brookings Papers on Economic Activity no. 2: 539-573.

BOOTH, A, D. R. JOHNSON, and H. M. CHOLDIN (1977) "Correlates of city crime rates: victimization surveys versus official statistics." Social Problems 25: 187.

BRADBURN, N. M., S. SUDMAN, and Associates (1979) Improving Interview Method and Questionnaire Design. San Francisco: Jossey-Bass.

CAMPBELL, D. T. and J. C. STANLEY (1966) Experimental and Quasi-experimental Designs for Research. Chicago: Rand McNally.

CANNELL, C. F. and R. F. KAHN (1968) "Interviewing," in G. Linzey and E. Aronson (eds.) Handbook of Social Psychology, vol. 2. Reading, MA: Addison-Wesley.

CARMINES, E. G. and R. A. ZELLER (1979) Reliability and Validity Assessment. Beverly Hills, CA: Sage.

CHERLIN, A. (1981) Marriage, Divorce, Remarriage. Cambridge, MA: Harvard University Press.

Chicago Tribune (1983) April 11: 1.

COALE, A. J. and F. F. STEPHAN (1962) "The case of the Indians and the teen-age widows," Journal of the American Statistical Association 57 (June): 338-347.

COLLINS, J. N. (1982) "Uses and limitations of 1977 Census of Governments Finance Data." Review of Public Data Use 10(May): 9-22.

COOK, T. D. and D. T. CAMPBELL (1979) Quasi-experimentation: Design and Analysis Issues for Field Settings. Chicago: Rand McNally.

COOK, T. D., L. DINTZER, and M. M. MARK (1980) "The causal analysis of concomitant time series" in L. Bickman (ed.) Applied Social Psychology Annual, vol. 1. Beverly Hills, CA: Sage.

Federal Bureau of Investigation (annual) Uniform Crime Reports. Washington, DC: Government Printing Office.

FOSSETT, J. W. and K. L. KRAMER (1981) "Urban revival, federal funds and the census: an assessment of federal data on cities," Prepared for delivery at the Midwest Political Science Association meetings, Cincinnati, OH, April 1981. (mimeo)

FUGUITT, G. V. and S. LIEBERSON (1974) "Correlation of ratios or difference scores having common terms," in H. L. Costner (ed.) Sociological Methodology. San Francisco: Jossey-Bass.

GORDON, A. C. and J. P. HEINZ [eds.] (1979) Public Access to Information. New Brunswick, NJ: Transaction Books.

GORDON, R. J. (1981) "The Consumer Price Index: measuring inflation and causing it." Public Interest (Spring): 112-134.

GROTH, P. G. (1982) "Values and the measurement of unemployment." Social Science Quarterly 63(March): 154-159.

JANDA, K. (1980) Political Parties: A Cross National Survey. New York: Free Press.

KALTON, G. (1983) Introduction to Survey Sampling. Beverly Hills, CA: Sage.

KELLEY, S. Jr., R. AYERS, and W. G. BOWEN (1967) "Registration and voting: putting first things first," American Political Science Review 61: 359-377.

KIM, J. O. et al. (1975) "Voter turnout among the American states." American Political Science Review 69: 107-131.

KISH, L. (1965) Survey Sampling. New York: John Wiley.

LANSING, M. (1974) "American woman: voter and activist," in J. Jaquette (ed.) Women in Politics. New York: John Wiley.

LONG, S. B. (1980) "The continuing debate over the use of ratio variables: facts and fiction," in K. F. Schuessler (ed.) Sociological Methodology. San Francisco: Jossey-Bass.

LYNN, N. (1979) "Women in American politics: an overview," in J. Freeman (ed.) Women: A Feminist Perspective. Palo Alto, CA: Mayfield.

McCLEARY, R. and R. A. HAY, Jr. (1980) Applied Time Series Analysis for the Social Sciences. Beverly Hills, CA: Sage.

MILLER, W. E., A. H. MILLER, and E. J. SCHNEIDER (1980) American National Election Studies Data Sourcebook, 1952-1978. Cambridge, MA: Harvard University Press.

MORGENSTERN, O. (1963) On the Accuracy of Economic Observations. Princeton, NJ: Princeton University Press. New York Times (1983) September 7: 12.

NIE, N. H. and J. RABJOHN (1979) "Revisiting mass belief systems revisited: or, doing research is like watching a tennis match." American Journal of Politcal Science 23: 139-175.

PALUMBO, D. J. (1977) Statistics in Political and Behavioral Science. New York: Columbia University Press.

PARKER, R. P. (1982) "The quality of the U.S. national income and product accounts." Review of Public Data Use 10(May): 1-8.

PENICK, B.K.E. and M.E.B. OWENS, III [eds.] (1976) Surveying Crime. Washington, DC: National Academy of Science.

POOLE, K. and H. ZEIGLER (1982) "Gender and voting in the 1980 presidential election." Presented at the annual meeting of the American Political Science Association, Denver, CO.

ROSENSTONE, S. J. and R. E. WOLFINGER (1978) "The effect of registration laws on voter turnout." American Political Science Review 72: 22-45.

RUSSETT, B. M., H. R. ALKER, Jr., K. W. DEUTSCH, and H. D. LASSWELL (1964) World Handbook of Political and Social Indicators. New Haven, CT: Yale University Press.

SCAMMON, R. A. et al. (annual) America votes. Washington, DC: Congressional Quarterly.

SCHUESSLER, K. (1974) "Analysis of ratio variables." American Journal of Sociology 80: 379.

SELLITIZ, C., L. S. WRIGHTSMAN, and S. W. COOK (1976) Research Methods in the Social Sciences. New York: Holt, Rinehart and Winston.

SHELLEY, L. (1979) "Soviet criminology After the revolution." Journal of Criminal Law and Criminology 70: 390-396.

SHISKIN, J. (1976) "Employment and unemployment: the doughnut or the hole?" Monthly Labor Review 99(Feb): 3-10.

SIMON, J. L. (1978) Basic Research Methods in Social Sciences. New York: Random House.

SKOGAN, W. G. (1981) Issues in the Measurement of Victimization. Washington, DC: Bureau of Justice Statistics.

———(1975) "Measurement problems in official and survey rates." Journal of Criminal Justice (Spring): 17-31.

SMITH, L. T. and P. E. ZOPF, Jr. (1976) Demography: Principles and Methods. New York: Alfred.

SOLZHENITSYN, A. (1969) Cancer Ward. New York: Farrar, Strauss = Giroux.

SULLIVAN, J. L. and S. FELDMAN (1979) Multiple Indicators. Beverly Hills, CA: Sage.

SULLIVAN, J. L., J. E. PIERESON, and G. E. MARCUS (1978) "Ideological constraint in the mass public: a methodological critique and some new findings." American Journal of Political Science, 22: 233-249.

———and S. FELDMAN (1979) "The more things change, the more they remain the same: rejoinder to Nie and Rabjohn." American Journal of Political Science 23: 176-186.

TAEUBER, R. C. and R. C. ROCKWELL (1982) "National social data series: a compendium of brief descriptions," Review of Public Data Use 10: 23-111.

TAYLOR, C. S. and M. C. HUDSON (1972) World Handbook of Political and Social Indicators, second edition. New Haven, CT: Yale University Press.

U.S. Bureau of the Census (1982-83) Statistical Abstract of the United States. Washington, DC: Government Printing Office.

———(1981) Statistical Abstract of the United States. Washington, DC: Government Printing Office.

———(1977) County and City Data Book. Washington, DC: Government Printing Office.

62

U.S. Congress, House of Representatives, Subcommittee on Census and Population (1980a) Hearings, Com. Serial 96-63.

———(1980b) Hearings, July 30.

———(1977) Hearings, Com. Serial 95-46.

U.S. Congress, House of Representatives, Subcommittee on Commerce, Consumers and Monetary Affairs (1980) Hearings, March 18.

U. S. Congress, House of Representatives, Subcommittee on State, Justice and Commerce (1976) Hearings, July 28-30.

U.S. Congress, Senate Committee on Governmental Affairs (1980) The Decennial Census: An Analysis and Review. 96th Congress, 2d Session.

U. S. Department of Justice (1979) National Crime Survey: Criminal Victimization in the United States: 1973-79. Washington, DC: Government Printing Office.

USLANER, E. N. (1976) "The pitfalls of per capita." American Journal of Political Science 20: 125.

WALH, R. C. (1982) "Is the Consumer Price Index a fair measure of inflation?" Journal of Policy Analysis and Mangement 1(Summer): 496-511.

WARWICK, D. P. and C. A. LININGER (1975) The Sample Survey: Theory and Practice. New York: McGraw-Hill.

HERBERT JACOB *is Professor of Political Science at Northwestern University. He received his Ph.D. from Yale University and previously taught at Tulane University, Johns Hopkins University, and the University of Wisconsin, Madison. He is past president of the Law & Society Association, and has been a Fellow at the Center for Advanced Studies in the Behavioral Sciences at Stanford University and at the Centre for Socio-Legal Research at Oxford University. He is editor of the* Law & Politics Book Review. *He has written widely on the American legal system. His most recent books are* Silent Revolution: The Transformation of Divorce in the United States *and* Law and Politics in the United States.

Printed in the United States
151122LV00002B/2/A

9 780803 922990